TROLLS

DO YOU BELIEVE?

This series features creatures that excite our minds. They're magical. They're mythical. They're mysterious. They're also not real. They live in our stories. They're brought to life by our imaginations. Facts about these creatures are based on folklore, legends, and beliefs. We have a rich history of believing in the impossible. But these creatures only live in fantasies and dreams. Monsters do not live under our beds. They live in our heads!

45th Parallel Press

Published in the United States of America by Cherry Lake Publishing
Ann Arbor, Michigan
www.cherrylakepublishing.com

Reading Adviser: Marla Conn MS, Ed., Literacy specialist, Read-Ability, Inc.
Book Design: Felicia Macheske

Photo Credits: © DM7/Shutterstock.com, cover; © LeksusTuss/Shutterstock.com, 1; © Pavelk/Shutterstock.com, 5; © Barandash Karandashich/Shutterstock.com, 7; © Dmitrijs Bindemanis, isoga/Shutterstock.com, 8; © Scott E Read/ Shutterstock.com, 11; © KathyGold/Shutterstock.com, 12; © AlexZaitsev/Shutterstock.com, 12; © Fotokostic/Shutterstock.com, 15; © Fernando Cortes/Shutterstock.com, 17; © StockCube/Shutterstock.com, 18; © Juan Aunion / Shutterstock.com, 21; © Vuk Kostic/Shutterstock.com, 22; © CatalinT/Shutterstock.com, 25; © RPBaiao/Shutterstock.com, 27; © Pics-xl/Shutterstock.com, 28

Graphic Elements Throughout: © denniro/Shutterstock.com; © Libellule/Shutterstock.com; © sociologas/Shutterstock.com; © paprika/Shutterstock.com; © ilolab/Shutterstock.com; © Bruce Rolff/Shutterstock.com

45th Parallel Press is an imprint of Cherry Lake Publishing.

Library of Congress Cataloging-in-Publication Data

Names: Loh-Hagan, Virginia, author.
Title: Trolls / by Virginia Loh-Hagan.
Description: Ann Arbor : Cherry Lake Publishing, 2017. | Series: Magic, myth, and mystery | Includes bibliographical references and index.
Identifiers: LCCN 2016031788| ISBN 9781634721509 (hardcover) | ISBN 9781634722827 (pbk.) | ISBN 9781634722162 (pdf) | ISBN 9781634723480 (ebook)
Subjects: LCSH: Trolls—Juvenile literature.
Classification: LCC GR555 .L65 2017 | DDC 398.21—dc23
LC record available at https://lccn.loc.gov/2016031788

Cherry Lake Publishing would like to acknowledge the work of The Partnership for 21st Century Skills.
Please visit *www.p21.org* for more information.

Printed in the United States of America
Corporate Graphics

TABLE of CONTENTS

Chapter One

Goat-Gobblers

**What are trolls? Where do they live?
What are the different types of trolls?**

"Who's crossing my bridge?" Trolls are famous for guarding bridges. In one story, three goats wanted to eat grass on the other side. They had to cross a bridge. A troll threatened to gobble them up. The goats tricked the troll. Each goat told the troll to wait for a bigger goat.

Trolls are dumb. But they're dangerous. They're powerful. They're evil monsters.

They live far away from humans. They live in dark places. They live under bridges. They live in mountain caves. They live in rocks. They live in forests. They come from countries close to Norway.

"The Three Billy Goats Gruff" is a popular fairy tale from Norway.

Real-World Connection

Sherry Groom loves trolls. She owns a large collection of troll dolls. She has a world record. She opened a museum. It's called the Troll Hole Art Emporium. It's in Ohio. It opened in June 2014. She has over 15,000 troll dolls and items. Her collection is displayed in two buildings. Groom got her first troll doll at age 5 for Christmas. She said, "I was fascinated by the tradition. My collection grew and grew. First, it was a bookshelf of trolls. Then, a basement full of extra trolls. Then, it grew into the idea that I was going to share them with the world." She created a storytelling nook. It has stools shaped like mushrooms. It has a troll cave. It has a troll bridge. It has a 10-foot (3 meters) troll mountain. During the summer, Groom dresses as Sigrid, the Troll Queen.

Trolls are **solitary**. They're loners. They're not really social. They don't talk much. But some do live in small **packs**. Packs are groups. They follow a leader. Each pack has a king and queen. They hunt together. They attack together.

They're **nocturnal**. They're active at night. They rest during the day.

They have powerful stomach juices. They can eat anything. They eat animals. They eat rocks. They eat trees. They eat metals. They eat trash. But their favorite food is humans. Some trolls eat other trolls.

Some trolls have plants and trees growing on them.

Some trolls are giants. These trolls are mountain or forest trolls. They smell really bad. They're hairy. They have long noses. They have large feet. They have large hands. They have jutting jaws. Their foreheads stick out. They have tough skin. Their skin looks like rocks. They may have **tusks**. Tusks are teeth that look like horns. Some only have one eye. Some have several heads. Some have tails.

Some trolls are smaller. They have stubby arms and legs. They have fat stomachs.

Some trolls look like humans. They're called **huldrefolk**. This means "hidden folk." They're beautiful. They have long cow tails.

Trolls come in different shapes and sizes.

Chapter Two

Troll Magic

How do trolls behave? How do they fight? What are their powers?

Female huldrefolk are **huldras**. Huldras are especially dangerous. They sing. They're beautiful. They charm human males. They turn humans into slaves. If they marry humans, they can become humans. But they lose their beauty. They're known as troll-wives.

Trolls are great thieves. They steal food. They kidnap human babies. They kidnap humans adults. They have the power to be invisible. They sneak into homes.

They're like animals. They take care of their basic needs. They get food. They get shelter. They're **territorial**. They guard their areas. Many trolls steal gold and gems. They protect their treasures.

Some trolls keep bears as pets.

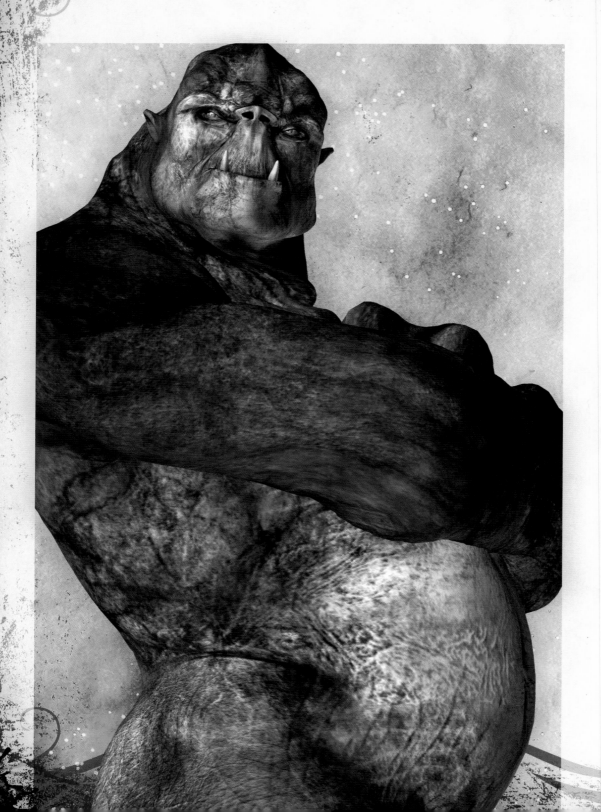

Trolls hate humans. Humans are only good for food. Trolls are violent fighters. They throw large stones. They use clubs. They use tree trunks. They smash humans. They throw up on humans. Their vomit eats flesh.

Trolls have a strong sense of smell. They can smell anything. They're hard to kill. Nothing pierces their skin. Only magical weapons can get through their skin.

Their breath has power. They breathe on food. They spoil the food. This makes humans sick. But it makes the food tasty to trolls. Their breath can also knock humans out.

Trolls use brute strength when fighting.

When Fantasy Meets Reality!

Trolls aren't the only creatures found under bridges. In 2012, Denise Ginley was walking by the Brooklyn Bridge. She found a carcass. A carcass is a dead animal body. The carcass was weird looking. It had a hairless body. It had a beak. It had a long tail. It had claws. It had five toes. It was missing its jaws. Ginley took pictures of it. She said, "It looked like the tide probably washed the carcass up there along with some driftwood." The creature has been called the East River Monster. Ginley said it looked like a bloated rat monster. Park officials thought it was a pig left over from a cookout. A university professor thought it was a dog. Some people thought it was a government lab experiment.

Even dragons respect trolls' powers.

Most trolls have **trolleri**. Trolleri is troll magic. It's powerful. It's intended to harm others. Trolls control humans' minds. They control humans' hearts. They control nature. They make thick fog. They resist other monsters' magic. They're **shapeshifters**. They change into animals. They change into humans. They lure humans to their homes. They make things **barren**. This means nothing can grow.

Trolls live for thousands of years. They can **regenerate**. They heal quickly. They regrow missing body parts. If they're really hungry, they eat their own body parts. They just grow new ones.

Chapter Three

Stoning Trolls

Why do trolls hate Christians? What are trolls' weaknesses?

Christians destroyed the trolls' powers. Humans started going to church. So, they stopped believing in trolls. They stopped being afraid of trolls. Trolls didn't like this. They felt disrespected. They took their anger out on Christians. Trolls hate Christians. They can smell their blood. They love eating them. So, they'll attack them.

Trolls hate the sound of church bells. This upsets them. They throw big rocks at churches. They try to destroy churches. They live far away from churches.

Christians can hurt trolls. They say their god's name. They use holy water. They show the cross. These things make trolls weak.

Norway was one of the last European countries to adopt Christianity.

Sunlight is the only way to stop a troll. Sunlight turns trolls into stone. Sometimes, it makes trolls explode. This is why trolls are nocturnal. Trolls are also afraid of lightning.

Trolls make things from stone or metal. They take care of themselves. But they're dumb at other things. Being dumb is their weakness. Trolls rely on being bullies. They can't rely on their brains. They're not clever. They can be tricked very easily.

Humans can trick trolls. They can take trolls' treasures. They use the treasures as a shield. This protects humans from harm. Trolls don't want to harm their treasures.

SURVIVAL TIPS!

- Be physically fit. Practice running. Be ready to escape. Don't try to fight trolls. Run away.

- Be fearless. Trolls smell fear.

- Know how to use weapons, especially a shield. Use the shield to protect yourself from the trolls' blows.

- Sniff the air for trolls. Look for their tracks on the ground. Avoid trolls. Stay out of their way.

- Don't be fooled by rocks. These could be trolls waiting for you. Be aware of everything around you.

- Don't let trolls know if you're Christian.

- Keep talking. Confuse trolls. Remember, trolls are dumb.

- Don't go out at night. If you do and you see a troll, distract him. Do this until sunrise.

Some troll hunters have been able to burn trolls alive.

Chapter Four

Viking Beginnings

Who is Bragi Boddason? What were Neanderthals? How were giants and trolls connected?

Troll stories started in Norway. They started in the early ninth century. Bragi Boddason was a Viking poet. He traveled. He told stories. He entertained kings and queens. He met a female troll. This was his most famous story. This was the first story about trolls. Boddason and the troll had a poem contest. The troll described herself. Boddason told a better poem. The troll let him escape.

Some people believe trolls came from **Neanderthals**. Neanderthals were a type of human.

They no longer exist. Trolls may be the last remaining Neanderthals. Their faces look the same.

The first known troll was a female.

Some people believe trolls came from the Jotun. Jotun were giants. They were called ice giants. They were enemies of the gods. They lived away from humans. They waited for the end of days. They battled against the gods.

Jotun lived before the universe was born. Ymir was the first Jotun. He had six heads. He had six arms. He had claws. He had fangs.

He was killed. His blood became the seas and rivers. His skull became the sky. His bones became mountains. His teeth became rocks. Trolls came from between his toes.

The Jotun are similar to the Titans from Greek myths.

Know the Lingo!

- **Bergtagna:** humans kidnapped and enslaved by trolls

- **Biergtrolde:** mountain trolls

- **Changeling:** baby troll that takes the place of a kidnapped human baby

- **Crag:** projecting part of a steep or rugged cliff

- **Fjord:** long, narrow body of water with steep sides or cliffs

- **Grotto:** cave

- **Ja:** Norwegian for "yes"

- **Knoll:** a small hill or mound

- **Nei:** Norwegian for "no"

- **Sjotrollet:** sea troll

- **Troldfolk:** troll folk

- **Trolla:** performing magic tricks

- **Trolldom:** folk magic

- **Trollkjerka:** troll's church

- **Trolltunga:** troll tongue

- **Vitterfolk:** trolls similar to huldrefolk

Chapter Five

Tricking Trolls

How did Troll Peaks form? Who is Fin? Who is Askeladden?

Trolls lived thousands of years ago. They hunted at night. They fought each other. There were two troll armies. They fought in a battle. The battle was bloody. They began at twilight. They forgot about time. They fought until sunrise. It was too late for them to run. The sun turned them into stone. They became Troll Peaks.

Troll Peaks are huge mountains. They're in central Norway. People believe they're troll **remains**. Remains are dead bodies.

Trold-Tindtern is Norwegian for Troll Peaks.

Explained by Science!

It takes millions of years to form mountains. Mountains are landforms. They rise higher than their surrounding areas. Earth has a crust. The crust is made of plates. These plates constantly move. There are different ways mountains are formed. In one way, the plates smash together. Two plates meet. Their edges crumple upward. Huge slabs of rock are pushed up into the air. These slabs become mountains. Another way is when plates meet and one plate lifts over the other plate. This action forms mountain ranges. In another way, volcano eruptions form mountains. Molten rock gets pushed up toward the surface. It cools. It becomes hard rock. In all cases, plates continue to push up against each other. This means mountains keep growing every day. They grow very, very slowly.

In many stories, humans must trick trolls. If they don't, they'll die. An example is Esbern Snare. Snare loved a girl. The girl's father wouldn't let them marry. He asked Snare to build a church. It was hard work. Snare asked a troll to help. They made a deal. Snare had to discover the troll's name. He had to do this before the church was finished. If he couldn't, the troll would take Snare's eyes and heart. The troll wanted them for toys for his baby. Snare had a hard time. Snare heard the troll's wife singing to her baby. Her song had the troll's name, Fin. Snare said, "Fin." He won.

Fin the troll tried to destroy the church when Esbern Snare discovered Fin's name.

Askeladden is in many Norwegian stories. Askeladden had two brothers. They were chopping wood. A troll scared off his brothers. Askeladden tricked the troll. He said he was really strong. He squeezed cheese. He told the troll the cheese was a rock. The troll got scared. He chopped wood for Askeladden. Askeladden kept teasing the troll. The troll did his work. He challenged the troll to an eating contest. Askeladden hid his food instead of eating it. He told the troll to cut a hole in his gut. He told the troll this would let him eat more. The troll did it. The troll died. Askeladden took the troll's treasures.

Trolls are dumb. But they're strong. Avoid them!

If you have a quick wit,
trolls can be easy to trick.

Did You Know?

- *Troll* is an old Norse word. It means "someone who walks clumsily."

- In traditional stories, trolls often say, "Fe, fi, fo, fum. I smell the blood of a Christian man."

- Norway has many places dedicated to trolls. Trollstigen is "Troll Ladder." It's a mountain road. Trollveggen is the "Troll Wall." It's the tallest vertical rock face in Europe.

- Some trolls have really long noses. Their noses get in their way when cooking. Trolls tuck their noses into their belts.

- One story features a really huge troll. The troll fishes for whales. He eats whales for dinner.

- Large mountain trolls are big. They look like rocks when sleeping. They have soil on their neck and shoulders. Pine trees grow from the soil.

- Norway has a lot of fishermen. Fishermen fish all day. They come to shore. They hang their mittens to dry. They keep children away from the pier. So, they told stories about trolls living in the fishermen's mittens.

- Trolls were popular in Scandinavia. They weren't popular in England. English stories features goblins instead of trolls.

- During the Middle Ages, Norway had special laws about trolls. People weren't allowed to wake trolls.

Consider This!

Take a Position: Trolls are presented as evil monsters. What makes them evil? Read other 45th Parallel Press books about monsters. Some people think trolls are the most evil of all the monsters. Do you agree or disagree? Argue your point with reasons and evidence.

Say What? Read the 45th Parallel Press book about fairies. Some people think trolls are a type of fairy. Explain how trolls are related to fairies. Explain the similarities and differences.

Think About It! J. R. R. Tolkien and J. K. Rowling are famous fantasy authors. They both feature trolls in their stories. They followed traditional beliefs about trolls. Their trolls are ugly. They're dumb. They fight. But the authors also added other details. Read stories about trolls. Why do authors add details about trolls? How do they combine traditional beliefs with new details?

Learn More

- D'Aulaire, Ingri, and Edgar Parin d'Aulaire. *D'Aulaires' Book of Trolls*. New York: New York Review of Books, 2006.

- Sautter, Aaron. *A Field Guide to Dragons, Trolls, and Other Dangerous Monsters*. North Mankato, MN: Capstone Press, 2015.

- Stewart, Gail B. *Trolls*. San Diego: Reference Point Press, 2011.

Glossary

barren (BAR-uhn) not fertile, not being able to grow

huldras (HUL-druhz) female huldrefolk

huldrefolk (HUL-druh-foke) type of trolls that look like humans except with a cow tail

Neanderthals (nee-AN-dur-thalz) species of humans that no longer exist

nocturnal (nahk-TUR-nuhl) active at night

packs (PAKS) groups that hunt and live together

regenerate (ree-JEN-uh-rayt) to heal or regrow limbs

remains (rih-MAYNZ) dead bodies

shapeshifters (SHAYP-shift-urz) creatures that can change their shapes

solitary (SAH-li-ter-ee) preferring to be alone; loner

territorial (ter-ih-TOR-ee-uhl) being very protective of space or of a specific area

trolleri (TRAHL-uh-ree) troll magic

tusks (TUHSKS) protruding teeth that look like horns

Index

About the Author

Dr. Virginia Loh-Hagan is an author, university professor, former classroom teacher, and curriculum designer. She hates Internet trolls, but she loves monster trolls. She lives in San Diego with her very tall husband and very naughty dogs. To learn more about her, visit www.virginialoh.com.